# REVERIE

DEAN MEREDITH

Copyright © 2017 Dean Meredith

ISBN: 978-1-925590-58-6
Published by Vivid Publishing
A division of Fontaine Publishing Group
P.O. Box 948, Fremantle
Western Australia 6959
www.vividpublishing.com.au

Cataloguing-in-Publication data is available from the National Library of Australia

All rights reserved. No part of this publication may be reproduced, stored in a retrieval system or transmitted in any form or by any means, electronic, mechanical, photocopying, recording or otherwise, without the prior written permission of the copyright holder. The information, views, opinions and visuals expressed in this publication are solely those of the author(s) and do not necessarily reflect those of the publisher.

**10.30 Exactly**

Bit sweaty
10.26 o'clock
Water falls
Light holds

Out of plonk
10.28 o'clock
Glass empty
Light holds

Front back
Front back
Consequences
And all that

He winces
Once only
Then smiles
Light holds

Casual pour
Plus two drops
Holds back
Consequences

Nose
Mouth
Body
Brain

**And then ...**

**Bio-WANK**

Raconteur, apparently
Provocateur, maybe
Clown prince of, improper
Juggler of vulgarities
Loser, extraordinaire
Pants, mostly up
Chicken thigh nibbler
Scribbler of sorts
Purveyor of, fine thoughts
Executor of (dis)taste
other aspects fade
a paisley mind
Conjuring mischief
Red rocking, luminously
like a fool
with a maybe
tomorrow, irreverent
Yeah, that could be it

## Canto 1

And Bathsheba did open up her shop for business
And running repairs although her long distant cousin
Covered and festooned with flowers of the sun
And yellow type all glowing in their apparent goldness
With petals and such soft and fragrant like exotic
And erotic in brackets oh no cross out that bit
It might upset the audience and we can't have that
Can we question mark now there's a thought
And what about the rest of the punctuation
There's a very long word with so many syllables
And plenty to rhyme with but nothing literary or
Substantial or great and dense such as Dylan Thomas
With all those words sounding thoughtful and thunderous
Or Sylvia Plath god bless her although even the deity
Himself would be loath to upset her above all
Poets female or male or somewhere in between
And the digression semantic and melancholic at once
Spat out all manner of manna from and to tops and
Bottoms and like Plath and Thomas at times cared not
For meaning and sense when so much of it was merely
Or mostly about words and sounds when really

The common men and women and bores thought
it might possibly be best if it could suggest facts
And feelings in terms of situations and real life
Not Persian carpets woven with myths too distant
For real folk to know let alone understand and that
Dear reader is all I have to say on the matter amen

**DEADLY**

ON THE BEACH
IT WAS BEAUTIFUL
WE WALKED AND TALKED
AND FORGOT EVERYTHING

WE LOOKED OUT AT THE WAVES
AND SHE WAS STUNNING BUT DEADLY
AND I NOTICED THE BOY IN THE SURF
AND THE FATHER SWIMMING TO SAVE HIM

SHE WAS DEADLY
WE SWAM, THE BOY, THE FATHER, AND ME
AND THE WAVES CRASHED THROUGH US
WHILE SHE LOOKED ON

HER LIPS WERE LIKE THE WAVES
AND HER MOUTH WAS LIKE THE SEA
I WANTED TO DIVE RIGHT IN
BUT I WAS AFRAID

SO SHE TEMPTED ME IN
SHE TEMPTED ALL OF US IN
THE BOY, THE FATHER, AND ME
SHE WAS DEADLY

**DENIAL**

TELL HER IF YOU DARE
THAT YOU NEVER EVER
WANT TO HAVE SEX WITH HER
AND WATCH THOSE EYES
THOSE DELIGHTFUL SUSPICIOUS
DISAPPOINTED EYES
WATCH THOSE FRIENDSHIP WANTING
TEAR FILLED LOVE FILLED EYES
TELL HER YOU WANT HER
BUT YOU NEVER EVER
WILL TOUCH HER IN THAT WAY
AND WATCH HER TROUBLED SMILE
AS SHE DIVIDES
SECURITY WITH INSECURITY
AND BEAMS HARD NIPPLED
BEHIND HER BLUSHING VEIL
LISTENING TO PROPAGANDA WORDS
WELL TAUGHT AND LEARNED
TO COVER HER FRAGILITY
TO COVER HER BEAUTY
TO COVER HER INNOCENSE
AND HER RECKLESS DESIRE
ALWAYS WANTING MORE
AND DENYING HERSELF
AS GOOD GIRLS SHOULD

## Earnestly Dreaming

He shows his worst
which are a few thoughts
and words

and she
not being stupid
sees that

But
What does she think?
He ernests

A man
Who can show his worst
As a warning

As a guide
She could do worse
He knew that too

In a dream
They came together
And in a dream
They stayed

**Fear Has Its Handmaidens**

His fleeting self-regard
Was like a faulty neon sign
In a sleazy city
Filled with candy mock repent

And every angel was his mother
Wanting him to save them
And every hooker was his mother
Wanting him to save them

His groin was like a forest
Full of wood and full of fire
And his hopeless history entwined him
With vines that grew to bind him

They wrapped and clung around his mass
Until his seeming end one up in sky
And then the slow dive down direct
Unto the ground of sucking soil and dread

Like locks they open for the fall
And dangle on their chain of lead
From air to ground and down until
Who knows when it all will end bone still

His angel his mother
The girl he dreamed of
His sister or brother
Nothing to see here nothing to fear

**Green**

Green is the color
Of a certain life
Of jumping fences
Of dreams beyond means

Green flies on flags
Of warring peoples
Combining so well
With other shades

Green sneaks up
Hammers my brain
Into something acceptable
Only to be shot down

Green is my wanting
More despite blessings
And subconsciously less
Because of shame

Green is the color
After water after rain
Catches light like no other
And turns it into beauty

Green takes me back
And moves me on
It's best friends and lovers
And jealousy in between

**Human**

You are known as human
Most advanced of the species
yet you don't have time
to listen to their stories
Numero Uno you are not
Looking down as much as up
You are not at the top
Nor the bottom, human
Just stuck in the middle
Like all of us, humans
Now you look up?

## If I Were Young Today

If I were young today:
I'd live rent free and sponge off my parents until I'm safely into middle age.
I'd be an Arts student and major in something important like Post Traumatic Stress resulting from troll abuse.
I'd adhere to one of the trendier forms of vegetarianism, surviving on a steady diet of nutritional shakes, dexamphetamine or crystal meth.
Killing and eating plants wouldn't be a problem, because to misquote Kurt Cobain – plants don't have any feelings.
I'd dream of stabbing both my parents for making me go to school and work, and not buying me the very latest I-Phone.
I'd have a beard, multiple piercings, large pink bow tattoos on the backs of my thighs, and a Butt-Plug.
I'd aspire to be a barista, burlesque performer, professional protester or meth cook.
I'd be asexual, atheistic, apolitical and amoral.
I wouldn't vote but if I absolutely had to it would obviously be for the Greens, Gay Alliance or Sea Shepherd.


If I were young today:
My only real friends would be my Facebook friends; my full photo album would be on INSTAGRAM; and my whole life story would be on Twitter.

My musical tastes would include Indi, Rap, and Hip-Hop. The Indi would be a bland mix of remixes mixed and looped together to all sound the same; and the Rap and Hip-Hop would consist of various Harlem and East LA gang codes interspersed with sampled beats and plenty of bling.

I'd not drive, but catch buses and trains instead; I'd avoid paying fares wherever possible, and refer to the drivers and guards as Fascists.

All of my communication would be via mobile phone; and all of my sex would be via Silly Selfie Cams.

My hair would be multi-coloured, permanently lacquered with product, and adorned with Christmas decorations.

I'd on occasion have a Skinny Latte, wear Skinny Jeans, and Slim Fit Shirts, even if I were a size XL; shoes would always be an optional extra.

Sometimes I'd wear stupid baseball caps that are too big for my great big head; and baggy trousers with no belt that I'd keep pulling up so they didn't fall down; and loud sports shoes costing a year's wages in a third world country; and still think I'm pretty fly in the Americanised mass market clone world, not so new not so edgy FASHIONISTA stakes.

My hero-persons would be the KARDASHIANS, Tim Minchin, Something Hyphen-HEIDKE; and the entire casts of *Game of Thrones* and *Girls*.

Most of my life would be spent online gaming and I'd regard my true self as an avatar.

I'd be extremely ultra-politically correct and completely non-judgemental about anyone or

anything.
In fact I'd be so politically correct and non-judgemental that I wouldn't really even exist.


If I were young today:
Instead of masturbating I'd self-harm twice a day; and if I were feeling particularly bored I'd also have a quick slash in the toilets at College, University or the Café.
Grammar for me would be the equivalent of Latin; and words would be spelled as they sound and as texts, including fashionable acronyms of the day, WTF!
I'd be a member of every minority group ever invented, and demand my fair share of victim status.
I'd wallow in my self-perceived misfortune; and blame every power elite and institution for my hopeless plight; except of course the Greens, Gay Alliance or Sea Shepherd.
I'd blog incessantly, upload insane rants like this one; use multi-media to post clips on YouTube; and seek ridiculous amounts for my 'narrative' via multiple crowd funding sources.
I'd have an App for everything; from brushing my teeth in the afternoon, to choosing my outdoor cinema experience that night.
I'd be an artist, regard BANKSY as a deity, go to trendy bars in alleyways, and hail UBER Taxis via one of my Apps.
I'd pretend the whole ride home to be on my mobile talking to my dad the Coffin Cheater, and tip the

driver with BITCOINS.
I'd know so much thanks to Wikipedia I'd think I was a deity just like BANKSY, and I'd be so cool and so bored and so broken and so lost I'd slash both wrists just for the fun of it, if it was 'In' and trending on Facebook - my death would go viral; imagine all those views and likes.

But I couldn't do that because it'd be too judgemental and politically incorrect, and worse still – it might get the 'thumbs down' from BANKSY.

**Lines**

The blade cuts through quite well
Silver strong and thin beyond
All denial of what it might do
Fine bone handle of disconnect

With minimal pressure it slides
Slow motion down an easy sell
Through the carve of disbelief
And guides a hand held true

Self ordained in silent reverie
Complaining not of lost regret
The deed is done with glee
Thought comes long after

Sharpness and pressure mix
Their sawing motion of intent
Separate and conquer still
Life and death like twins

Leave breath to float
And find a neck to feel
Before the severing
As inward drive relents

She keys no invitation
Nothing more is meant
Until in hyper dreams
We meet without repent

**Liquid Gold**

He was greyer than grey
Whiter than white
He was up looking down
In looking out

His mushroom cloud
Tasted like honey
His magic forest
Forbidden ground

Two fairy nymphs
Haunted his dreams
Fingers smelling
… Like poison

Devils' nectar
Dripped from the tree
And he was tempted
… Impossibly

**Looking Good**

She was death brightened up
With interest
White beyond the pale
Red lipstick
A soul I could only imagine
Glorious
In its unfathomable depths
Dark
As a contrast dye
Her lure
Central to our swim around
Beguiled
Even the sharks hesitate
Denying
Their million year twitch
Unknowable
Her frenzied passion attack
Relentless promise
Hell imagined, probably untrue
Nonetheless
Clichés remain unreal
Oh to die
In her ghostly clutch

**Loose Bit of Fluff**

A loose bit of fluff
Blew across my grass
Then it got stuck there
Nothing let it pass

That fluff was you
The grass is me
You will fly off
Eventually

But I'll grow on
Toward the sky
Until I'm cut
And then I'll die

And you'll blow on
Soft and carefree
Until you find
Another me

And I'll be dead
And thrown away
And you'll blow on
To another day

Then I'll be tipped
Back on the ground
And I'll blow too
It goes around

And we'll blow on
And never stay
And we'll blow on
But never stay

**Loyal Subjects**

What day is it?
What month is it?
What number is it?

Kings are fucked
with wanton intent
No pressure

Dress to the floor
No knickers
Curly red quiff

a royal taster
sniffs the air
all most acceptable

Invisible time traveller
Takes a selfie
Incommunicado

His whore enjoys
What she can
For the realm

**Lucid Dreams**

No distractions
She comes again
I wish it was me
The smell of smoke

Left to ourselves
We reach out
Impossibly for something
To begin again

The music washes
Through and over
Once more we are
Alone with our sins

The random bites
Teeth marks within
Hunters circle
Prey from above

How we scurry
How we scamper
Crazy little minds
Dreaming of love

The smell of smoke
I wish it was me
She comes again
No distractions

**Making Ends**

My fade glowed on
In its half-life
Of seething fluorescence
Barely a knowing pulse

My rock hard cocked
And full of reasoning
Saw nothing but sky
With one more chance

A beckoning slut star
Cut her way through
Part of a secret wish
She bore me down relentless

And my lizard slid out
From beneath his very best
Naked amidst the covers
Of blonde angel night

She bit me and sunk off
Like a shadow on the run
It hurt burned down got up
Cried out in weeping fear

Her crippled bend shimmy
Lost on my pointless soul
She saw me gone
I watch her still

**MÉNAGE À TREE**

THEY WERE BOTH DEAD ROOTS
BUT I'D ALWAYS PLANTERSIZED
ABOUT A TREESOME

**Missing Something**

I asked myself
"What do I have to give?"
And the voice inside was silent

So I waited
For an answer
And still there came nothing

I wondered
If the voice had gone
And where it might be

Pondering
As I've always done
Would it ever come back?

I decided
to be very quiet
In case it was trapped

and hoping
to hear it again
my breathing slowed

Down
I went
and followed

## Miss Sulphur

I liked the irony
Of her mind body politic
The self-exploitation
Flirting with our souls

I liked the seeming contradictions
Of her force field fluff
Dancing through the landmines
Too fast for serious damage

I liked the inconsistencies
Of her pussy-power thoughts
And the shrapnel spray
That came with it

She was big-bang theory
In Pandora's Box
She was a mini A-bomb
Searching for a trigger

She was Redhead Matches
Looking for a fuse
For her, size was only matter
And everything was relative

For me, what I saw
And what I heard
Were two of the same?
It was all energy and light

She was an atom
Splitting apart
A blinding flash
Of nuclear art

**MY DEFINITION OF OPTIMISM**

I'M LOOKING FORWARD
TO THE YOUNG SCANDINAVIAN GIRLS
WAITING ON MY PORCH
TO FUCK ME
BUT FIRST
I NEED TO GET A PORCH

**My Space or Yours**

She was the exception
To most of my rules
By the time she ushered me up
Like a wild brumby
Half wanting to be tamed
By the time her eyes pierced mine
By the time her liquid mouth
Reached for mine
It was too late
And not late enough

For a miracle
For a flood
We traced and scanned each other
Like two 3D printers
Sculpting wishes
Making something real
With fakery and witchcraft
After the bodies, the minds
Those deep dark voids like black holes
Sucking everything around them in

**No Place like Rome**

She
Truly beautiful
Lies on her back
In submission mode

He
Truly stupid
Lies on his back
In begging mode

They
Are both
Of the same skin
Taught to obey

We
Follow
Seeming truths
Fearing if we stray

All
Do as they think
Hoping for something more
So far so good

The sinner sinks
Into his own despair
Created by him and no other
And he is happy there

**Not One More**

Lost on two sides
Of the same thing
We caught each other
Questioning
Ridiculous
Matters of consequence
Her brandied top
One freckle in sight
"I thought you'd never ask"
She said
My day glowed
Birthdays I think
Yes
Birthdays

**Ode to Faye Dunaway**

I want Faye Dunaway
I don't know why
I don't know what for
I just want her
She appeals to me
My kind of woman
Don't ask
I'm not going to explain
She'd hate that
I'd hate that
Explanations for everything
Some things are unexplainable
They're better that way
A little mystery
Some humanity
Some doubt
That's what we all need
To be a little unsure
Of everything
Including ourselves
Let the contradictions flow
Embrace the hypocrisy
Even forgive the odd lie
If it's for a good cause
Forgive your lover
Forgive yourself
Love your forgiver
Hope she's Faye Dunaway
And if she's not
So what

Love her anyway
As if she was

**Oh Charlotte**

As soon as now
I caught myself
Thinking of her
The punishment
Was supposed to be over
Like wine on a Monday
I had no escape
From whatever she spun
Stuck fast for sure
She plucked her web
Crescent nails and the dull screech
Of her death harp up high and shrill
Not much more than that really
Cross my heart
Yeah she's coming for that too
Don't say I didn't warn you
What the fuck are you saying?
She let me know I'm not forgotten
But will be one day
All eight of her eyes looked hard at me
Like I was supper, but the night was young
She tapped her string
As a hint, as a gesture
A kind of love
I soiled myself, threw up
She didn't seem to mind
Not a twitch, eight eyes looked on
Those were my last thoughts

**On My Bonnet**

Day month 37
Fly by manic
Burn me in
Thorns precipitate
Thoughtful murder
Crown someone
Upstart
Entice me blind
Erect nippled
Blouse undone
Shoot me down
Passion kitten
Pants on fire
Impossible waist
Upmarket
Rough wanting
Free trade
Simple gold
Sandals
Soft leather
Neatly bound
I'm not around
As you like it
I never
Really was

**P.J. Mouse**

She liked her men
Thin and tall
She liked their penises
Long and thin
Like rats
Up her drainpipe
Vermin
Are people too

Secretly
I offered
To lick
Her silky thighs
Inside out
No tongue tip
But a carpet bombing
With collateral quiver

Her Minnie Mouse
Everything
Entranced
My cartoon brain
Which villain?
Will I be
I'm no Mickey
Maybe a brute

Yeah

She might
Just like that

## Shooters

Every bullet was made by a mind
And every bullet was shot by a heart
And every bullet was hit or miss
And every bullet was in or out
And every shell changed something
And every shell was cold and hot
And every shell was smooth and rough
And the hands that held them
And the hands that fired them
And the eyes that saw them
And the bodies that felt them
Were distant no matter how close
Were shameful no matter how clothed
Were sorry no matter how righteous
Were wanting no matter how complete

**Sister Mary**

Don't exaggerate
You jerk
Just describe me
As I am
As I really am

No pressure again
Let me raise my head
Above your knees
I'm not clearing my nostrils
You know

With her
I am beggar
Warrior
Saint
Misanthrope

Pinkness
Surrounds
Entraps
Squeezes out
My hate

Her pinkness
My Magdalene
Crucify me
Witness the escape
Come with me

## Sliding Down

Skidding
Down the smooth clay terraces
Of love
On my arse
She licked her lips once
I noticed
She noticed me noticing
We both liked it
I like it more than her
But I'm older
She laughs off my stereotype
I adore her for it
Down the slopes I slide
Love is everywhere
She says, "hey fool
How has all that ...
Head over heart gone for you? "
I naturally thought of Hobbes
"Nasty, brutish and short"
She licked her lips once more
I noticed again
She saw me etcetera
was I pushed?
Who saw who coming?
I'm focused on her lips
She knows it too
She's no fool like me
her focus is the next adventure
Go figure...

**Slow Suicide**

In my grandmother's house
Which I bought cheap
With my hard earned
Sold soul credit
I've lived like a loner
With my family
At times
My beautiful family
Never giving up
Them on me
Me on them
Always scarred
Always scared
Of losing it
My privacy
My individuality
My freedom
Here I am
In this house
All of us
Slowly dying
Too slow
Too fast
For me

**Sneaky**

He takes another chance
on no sure thing
but a hope and a maybe
like a spiritual man
whose spirit is unbroken
she sees his thoughts
and likes them
in her mirror mind
of silver and shadow
what of the light?
Everything
to be sure

**Such a Fine Girl**

You were the girl
The very young girl
Who offered me an egg
When my belly was empty
The same girl
The very same girl
Who my crazy friend offended
Because he knew no better
And then much later
You were the girl
The amazing girl
Who strummed her guitar
And sang so beautifully
Like heaven itself
In the stony night
In the balmy night
With light shining coy
In your smiling presence
In your smiling eyes presence
With an angel voice
And no pretension
And no fucking pretension
Just beauty in the night
And all our silent adoration
Counting for nothing
Counting for everything
All of us lost
And together
Silent joy in the haze

And you so great
And shy and gay
And me in awe
Almost silently

## Sweet Relief

Her husband
The landlord
Lay on their bed
Large and plump
Quite dead
She brushed her hair
Naked
With her back to him
Admiring herself
In the mirror
His hands huge
Like every part of him
She fair
And fine figured
Fireplace empty
Two ornamental cats
On the mantle
She seemed contented
He seemed relieved

**Terror Within**

The world is fucked
Officially, unofficially
Literally or not
Screwed, up, in, out

The thread is broken
Things don't work
People don't work
We're still slaves

The world is fucked
Life is war
Slow, fast
And corrupt

The ink is dry
Art imitates art
Wankers wank
In public secrecy

The world is fucked
Hope fades
Like fashion
Ugliness pokes through

The tin is empty
Our souls dead
Dreaming we're alive
No, just dying

The world is fucked
And all within it
Human misnomers
Animals too

The bombs are falling
Times are ending
Clocks will stop
Words will go

**The Best Deaths Are Silent**

Boredom
It's a killer
Untapped potential
On both sides

Celluloid crawls through
Unstoppable despite the failures
Of power, of various unnamed parts
Light sources come and go and come again

Eventually everything stands still
Despite the growing lines
Backed up, falling out
One day follows

The next is
Not enough
But no
It was

**The Imperfect Couple**

Where are you at? He thought
wondering what your friends might think
about me, about us

where are you at? She thought
Wondering about the sex or lack thereof
Maybe positions and such

Yeah that's where I'm at she thought
My friends are important to me
And most of them don't want my body

Yeah that's where I'm at he thought
Sex is important to me
It's how I love

We're no good for each other
They both thought
With regret

Looking at their mobiles
Hoping for a message
To change their minds

**Uncertain Numbers**

Greetings
I am one of the sons
One of the scribes
Offspring of our deities
Wanting to do good
Out to impress

The run in her tights
Had her immediate attention
Words flowed in
She had been listening
After all
Caught your eye and everything

Respect her powers
Admire the mind
Fear her beauty
Cuteness approaching infinity
Dance with me
She casually demanded

I moved awkwardly
Rearranged my lunatic fringe
Particles joyous
Helpless
In her spell

**Welcome Aboard**

Pretty
Fucking
Wasted
Flaps up

All aboard
Don't mind me
This is your Captain
Speaking

Rest assured
You are in good hands
This aircraft is well serviced
And the attendants first class

Leaving the runway
We will maintain our positions
High above the clouds
Until they tell us to come down

Should things start flashing
And alarms begin to sound
Do not despair
We are insured

## Where Does It Hurt?

Her neon press
And my calculated consumption
She made off with something
No matter
It will show itself
In the wanting
Horror shows and such
She made off with my best bits
They went willingly let it be said
Horny in the mornings
It's a condition
Nurse!

**Who Would Have Guessed?**

He stood in the kitchen
Drank his coffee
Pressed the toaster down again
For the third or fourth time
Toasted his crumpets
When they popped up
They smelled brown, slight burn
Golden, hard and delicious
The bullet travelled silently
Splashed through the back window
Into his head and out the other side
Embedding deep in the splintered cupboard

His life flashed up on the screen
For all to see, no ratings or warnings
Just thrust up there for all to see
The platitudes, the progressives
Something to hope for, Rainbow Party
Rock on, exclamation mark!
"Where the FUCK were you?" I was
on another job, yeah that's it
did I say that or just think it?
Is this *The Simpsons*?
Me on *The Simpsons*
Who would have guessed?

www.ingramcontent.com/pod-product-compliance
Lightning Source LLC
Chambersburg PA
CBHW061515040426
42450CB00008B/1627